I've Got the One~More~ Washload Blues...

I've Got the One-More-Washload Blues...

by Lynn Johnston

Andrews and McMeel, Inc.

A Universal Press Syndicate Company

Kansas City • New York • Washington

ISBN: 0-8362-1166-9

Library of Congress Catalog Card Number: 81-68248

People ask me when I started drawing — and I have to say that I've always drawn.

They ask me why I draw cartoons and the only answer is that it feels good. It feels great, in fact.

It's always been easier for me to joke about things that worried me than to come right out and describe them — and when I discovered that I could describe things with lines — and that my descriptions were funny — I was hooked on the drug of approval, forsaking all other artforms to "study," if you will, the art of humorous illustration.

Most people don't joke enough about things that worry them — and parenting must be one of the biggest sources of worry of all time. Or call it insecurity. And then there's the guilt! What do we feel when we holler at the kids? Our mates? The neighbor with the stereo? Guilt! Who in this world could ever follow all the sage advice in all those parenting books and be human? We put unreasonable demands on ourselves sometimes and wind up feeling guilty.

I started letting some of this guilt flow out onto my drawing board — therapy, you could call it — and to my utter amazement, I discovered that others actually identified with me.

When I started to draw the hunched and disheveled housewife, eyebags drooping, mop in hand, grimacing as she removes junior from the dog's dish, I am cleansed. When I trace the profiles of small children — beaming as they mash canned pears into the piano — I am somehow relieved. My spirits soar as I stipple the chin of a husband roused from slumber by something that smells awful in the hall. All the frustrations and worries of the day, I can store for a while — and then I let them explode on paper. There's a need to express the loving things that happen too, and with just a few lines, a feeling or an impression can be turned into comic relief.

I know I'm lucky. As well as being able to draw, I inherited the gift of a sense of humor. Thank you, Mom and Dad. These gifts have saved me.

I want to dedicate this "diary" to you, to the folks at Universal Press Syndicate, and to the many young parents who have written to me.

I've been allowed the freedom to talk non-stop to a million people — and you're telling me I'm normal! Thank you.

Lynn Johnston

11

I WASN'T DOIN' ANYTHIN'... MUCH... WELL... LAWRENCE WAS WALKIN' THE FENCE... AN' THERE WAS A BIG PUDDLE... AN'... AN'...

HE SORT OF FELL OFF... ER... I GUESS I KIND OF HELPED HIM FALL OFF... AN'... WELL... HE PUT A GOB OF MUD ON MY HEAD—

...SO... WELL... I SORT OF PUT A GOB OF MUD ON HIS HEAD... AN' HE TOLD HIS MOM... AN' HIS MOM YELLED A WHOLE BUNCH AN' I CAME HOME.

YESSIR... THEY CAN'T ESCAPE THE OL' "STARE OF TRUTH!"

BELIEVE ME... I DON'T THINK YOU'RE FAT!

HOW CAN I CONVINCE YOU THAT YOU'RE JUST RIGHT?

BESIDES... I'VE ALWAYS LIKED HEALTHY WOMEN...

AAAAHHH

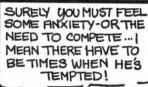

HOW CAN I KNOW WHAT THE MATTER IS - IF YOU DON'T TELL ME!

WOULD YOU STOP THINKING AT ME LIKE THAT!

THERE WAS A TIME WHEN I COULDN'T WAIT TO GET MARRIED.

THEN I COULDN'T WAIT TO HAVE A HOUSE OF MY OWN. THEN... FOR CHILDREN, - I COULDN'T WAIT!

..NOW THAT I HAVE ALL THE THINGS I COULDN'T WAIT FOR - & CAN DECIDE WHAT & WHO I WANT TO BE....

I'VE GOT TO WAIT.

HAVE YOU LOOKED AFTER THIS WOMAN YET, JAKE?

..THAT YOUR WAGON OVER THERE, MA'AM?

HOW DID THE BARBER KNOW YOU WAS A MISSUS, HEY, MOM?... MOM? MOM?

WOMAN...MA'AM...MRS... WHAT EVER HAPPENED TO "YOUNG LADY"?

16

WHAT WE NEED AS HOMEMAKERS IS TO BE APPRECIATED!

KIDS NATURALLY TAKE US FOR GRANTED.—WE MUST GET OUR THANKS FROM OTHER SOURCES!

HI, EL—I'M HOME!

SLAM

WHAT DIDN'T I DO THIS TIME?

I DO APPRECIATE WHAT YOU DO AROUND HERE!

I COME HOME TO A CLEAN HOUSE, GOOD FOOD, WELL MANAGED FINANCES & HAPPY KIDS...

BUT I ADMIT THAT I FIND IT HARD TO SEE HOW THE HOUSE & KIDS CAN OCCUPY YOUR EVERY WAKING MINUTE.

WHAT DO YOU DO ALL DAY, ELLY?

MICHAEL!.. DON'T YOU EVER LET ME HEAR YOU USING THOSE WORDS AGAIN!!!

'MON, LAWRENCE, LET'S GO OVER TO THE PARK...

SHE CAN'T HEAR A THING FROM THERE...

19

HEY, MA! I FINISHED DIGGING OUT THE PUMPKIN!

WHERE DO YA WANT ME TO PUT THE GUCKY STUFF?

GIVE UP, TWIRG! YOUR PLANET IS SURROUNDED BY MY SPACE PATROL!

SOMETIMES I THINK I'VE FORGOTTEN HOW TO FANTASIZE, ... HAVEN'T YOU, JOHN?

... JOHN?

TRICK OR TREAT!

JUST A MINUTE ... I'D BETTER MAKE SURE THIS STUFF IS SAFE ...

MUNCH

YOU CAN NEVER TRUST ANYTHING (MUNCH SLURP) HOMEMADE ...

IT'S A GOOD THING YOUR DAD CAME ALONG, MIKE ...

ALREADY HE'S SAVED US FROM 4 POPCORN BALLS, TWO TAFFY APPLES AND 6 CHUNKS OF HOMEMADE FUDGE.

20

MICHAEL HAS JUST BEEN AWFUL LATELY, CONNIE— HE'S RUDE AND DISOBEDIENT AND MEAN TO EVERYONE...

HE USES BAD LANGUAGE, HE ABUSES HIS TOYS —& I THINK WE'VE REALLY TRIED OUR BEST!

I LOVE MY SON, CONNIE... I JUST DON'T **LIKE** HIM VERY MUCH.

SCIENTIFICALLY BLENDED EMOLLIENTS PENETRATE DRY SKIN LINES....TO LIFT & SEPARATE—

WHEN THOSE TELL-TALE CREASES BEGIN TO SHOW —*Fountain of Youth* IS GUARANTEED

THE MIRACLE DISCOVERY FOR AGING SKIN... *No one will guess you are over 30!*

I'M BUYING THIS FOR A FRIEND.

WOW. SHE'S GOT GREAT TEETH...

HI, LIZZIE...

GWONG!

WHAP

YOU LITTLE RAT!

MICHAEL! HOW MANY TIMES HAVE I TOLD YOU NOT TO BE MEAN TO YOUR BABY SISTER!

I TOLD ELLY TO TAKE OFF THIS WEEKEND... AND LET ME TAKE THE KIDS FOR A CHANGE.

I FIGURE SHE NEEDS A BREAK.

YOU'RE A NICE GUY, DR. PATTERSON.

I'M A SAINT.

HAVE A GREAT VISIT, HONEY... WE'LL BE FINE!

..THINK I'LL CHECK OUT THE PAPER WHILE THE KIDS AMUSE THEMSELVES.

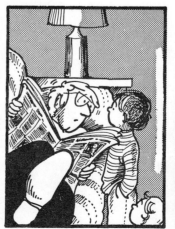

..IS IT FOOLISH OF ME TO ASK FOR A FEW MINUTES TO MYSELF?

WHERE DOES MOM KEEP THE SPAGHETTI, MICHAEL?

WHERE DID MOM PUT LIZZIE'S CLEAN PANTS?

HOW AM I SUPPOSED TO KNOW WHERE HER BOTTLE IS!!

I JUST LIVE HERE...

I HAD A GREAT TIME WITH MY FOLKS, JOHN!

MY MOTHER ALWAYS GIVES ME CONFIDENCE. SHE MAKES ME SEE THE BEST IN LIFE!

GOOD OL' MOM... SO, WHAT SAGELY ADVICE DID SHE IMPART? WHAT WORDS OF WISDOM?

SHE CALLED ME A SPOILED BRAT.

WELL, DOC... I SEE YOU SURVIVED BEING A HOUSEHUSBAND!

SO... AREN'T YOU GOING TO RAVE ON ABOUT THE DISHES, THE LAUNDRY, THE FLOORS & THE MESS?

THAT STUFF NEVER BOTHERED ME, JEAN...

I LEFT IT ALL FOR ELLY.

27

GOOD GRIEF! ···CAN I BELIEVE WHAT I'M SEEING?

THE FLOOR WAS DIRTY··· SO I'M WASHING IT!

WE'VE ALWAYS BEEN HONEST WITH EACH OTHER, HAVEN'T WE, JOHN?

ARE YOU DOING ME A FAVOR OR TRYING TO MAKE ME FEEL GUILTY?

COME ON, MA ···GET UP. IT'S MORNING, MA!

:GRRUMPH:- I DON'T WANT TO GET UP, MICHAEL ··GO GET A (YAWN) GLASS OF MILK···

YOU CAN'T STAY IN BED··· I'LL BE LATE FOR SCHOOL, AN'LIZZY IS SOAKIN' WET!

IF I WERE WIDE AWAKE·· I'D THINK MY 6 YEAR OLD WAS TREATING ME LIKE A 6 YEAR OLD····

Oo

CONNIE SAYS I DON'T APPRECIATE YOU ENOUGH, JOHN···

SHE SAYS I DWELL ON PETTY PERSONAL PROBLEMS & OVERLOOK THE REALLY WORKING PARTNERSHIP WE HAVE···

WHUMPH

BUT I GUESS I'D KNOW IF OUR MARRIAGE WAS SUFFERING···

29

YOU KNOW, ELLY... YOU ARE GETTING A LITTLE ROTUND.

OH, YEAH?... AND WHAT DO YOU CALL THIS STUFF?

THAT'S DIFFERENT. ON MEN, A LITTLE EXTRA WEIGHT LOOKS OK!

THERE'S NO JUSTICE IN A SOCIETY WHERE WOMEN GET FAT... AND MEN GROW "LOVE HANDLES"...

HOWCOME GROWNUPS KNOW MORE THAN KIDS.... HOWCOME THEY'VE GOT ALL THE ANSWERS?

IT'S SORT OF WEIRD HOW THEY'RE ALL SMARTER THAN US....

FROM DOWN HERE... THEIR HEADS LOOK SO SMALL.

THIS IS IT, TED... IT'S FINALLY HAPPENED...

LYNN JOHNSTON

AFTER ALL THIS TIME.. & ALL WE'VE BEEN THROUGH ...SHE'S LEAVING ME.

I TRIED TO TREAT HER WELL... I THOUGHT I'D GIVEN HER EVERYTHING!

WHERE AM I GOING TO FIND ANOTHER HYGIENIST LIKE MARIE?

36

40

WHO LEFT THE ☆!@ SCREWDRIVER ON THE STAIRS?

YOU DID.

THEN FOR HEAVEN'S SAKE TELL ME TO BE MORE CAREFUL!

PICK THIS UP! SNIVEL PUT THAT AWAY SNIFF SNIFF DO THIS... DO THAT!...

WORK! WORK! WORK!... NOBODY LOVES MEEEE...!!

DO THIS! SNIVEL DO THAT! OOOOH. NOBODY LOVES MEEEE...

41

For Better or For Worse

By Lynn Johnston

IT'S UNFAIR!

I CAN'T STAND IT ANY MORE!!!

NOBODY DOES ANYTHING AROUND HERE BUT ME! — EVERYBODY JUST DROPS THEIR STUFF FOR ME TO PICK UP!

I'M SICK SICK SICK OF PICKING-UP...

MFFF!

WHAT WAS THAT?

YOU SNICKERED!

HONEST, ELLY.. I COULDN'T HELP IT..(GIGGLE)..YOU LOOK SO FUNNY WHEN YOU'RE MAD!

WHUMP!

DO YOU THINK SHE EXPECTS US TO PICK THIS UP?

45

CLOGG CLICKA TICKA SCRAPE

?!?

ALRIGHT! WHO STUFFED THE OREO IN MY TYPEWRITER!

I DON'T WANT TO CLEAN UP THIS PLACE...

IT'S A DUMP...BUT I HAVE NO INCENTIVE.

WHATCHA DOIN', MOM?

INVITING SOMEONE CRITICAL OVER FOR DINNER....

WHAT MAKES YOU SO DOGGONE GOOD ALL THE TIME, 'LIZABETH?

ALL YOU DO IS CRAWL AROUND ALL DAY BEING ICKY-CUTE!

YOU NEVER GET INTO TROUBLE!

SIGH ... GIVE HER TIME.

48

I DON'T WANT TO GO TO WORK THIS MORNING ...

—NOW, WOMEN ARE LUCKY BECAUSE THEY DON'T HAVE A STRUCTURED DAY. THEY HAVE A CHOICE ...

YEAH. GOOD POINT. NOW ... SHOULD I SCOUR THE TOILETS BEFORE I FOLD THE LAUNDRY ... OR VICE VERSA?

HOW CAN I WALK TO KINDERGARTEN, MA— IT'S FREEZING OUT THERE!

IT'S THREE WHOLE BLOCKS AWAY! ... I'LL DIE!

MICHAEL, WHEN I WAS YOUR AGE, I WALKED 6 BLOCKS TO SCHOOL AND WE DIDN'T EVEN OWN A CAR!

... AND I SWORE I'D NEVER SOUND LIKE MY MOTHER.

UGH! .. IT'S ABOUT TIME I CLEANED OUT THIS FRIDGE!

ONE CUP NONDESCRIPT GRAVY, A BOWL OF (SNIFF) CUSTARD, ONE SLICE BOLOGNA, A MUSHY GREEN PEPPER ...

I FEEL GUILTY THROWING OUT ALL THIS STUFF ....

MY MOTHER WOULD HAVE MADE IT INTO A CASSEROLE.

WHAT'S THIS BOTTLE OF CHANGE FOR, ELLY?

CHINKA CUNK

ER, WELL... I SAVE IT FROM THE GROCERIES SO I CAN SPEND IT ON... OH... LITTLE THINGS I NEED.

BUT, HONEY, YOU KNOW THAT I'LL GIVE YOU MONEY FOR WHATEVER IT IS YOU NEED. ALL YOU HAVE TO DO IS ASK!

I KNOW... BUT THIS WAY I FEEL I'VE EARNED IT.

THIS IS IT. FOR THE FIRST TIME IN TWO YEARS, I AM WILLINGLY GOING TO MISS IT!

THERE. TWO AND A HALF MINUTES BEFORE "SUDDEN ILLNESS" COMES ON...

THIRTY SECONDS TO GO...... I GIVE UP!!

...NO HUMAN CAN STAND THE AGONIES OF SOAP OPERA WITHDRAWAL!

I'VE GOT TO STOP. I'VE GOT TO BREAK THE HABIT!!

I SPEND AN HOUR EVERY DAY WATCHING INANE, REPETITIVE DRIVEL.

SOAP OPERAS ARE IMPOSSIBLY DEPRESSING, INSULTING, AND A WASTE OF TIME...

THEY'RE ALSO FATTENING.

GUESS WHAT, LAWRENCE ···MY MOM LET ME WALK ALL THE WAY HERE BY MYSELF!

ELLY···IF YOU DIDN'T KNOW I HAD LAWRENCE···

WOULD YOU SAY THAT I LOOKED SINGLE?

I'D SAY YOU LOOKED LIKE AN ATTRACTIVE GIRL, PAST HER TWENTIES.

I LOOK DIVORCED AND ON THE MAKE, DON'T I?

IT'S TRUE, ELLY··ONCE YOU'RE DIVORCED, IT'S HARD NOT TO LOOK THE PART.

YOU TAKE YOUR KID TO THE PARK, ALONE···AND TRY NOT TO LOOK FOR MEN WHO ARE THERE WITH THEIR KIDS··· ALONE.

HEY·· WHAT HAPPENS IF YOU DO SEE A GUY ALONE IN THE PARK WITH HIS KIDS?

BESIDES SENDING LAWRENCE OVER WITH POPCORN, SHOWING OFF MY RINGLESS LEFT HAND AND SMILING A LOT··· NOTHING.

ONCE YOU'RE NOT PART OF A COUPLE, MOST OF YOUR MARRIED FRIENDS DRIFT AWAY...

WELL, NOTHING'S CHANGED FOR ME, CONNIE... WE'VE KNOWN EACH OTHER FOR 10 YEARS!

THANKS, ELLY. YOU'RE ONE OF THE FEW HAPPILY MARRIED FRIENDS I'VE GOT.

...IT SORT OF MAKES YOU WONDER... WHICH ONE OF US IS IN THE MINORITY GROUP.

CONNIE FIGURES THAT YOU AND I HAVE A NEAR PERFECT RELATIONSHIP...

SHE SAYS... OF ALL THE COUPLES SHE KNOWS, OURS IS A REAL WORKING MARRIAGE!

I'LL BUY THAT...

I'VE NEVER WORKED SO HARD IN MY LIFE.

CONNIE IS RIGHT— I'VE BEEN TAKING OUR MARRIAGE FOR GRANTED!

MAYBE I NEED A CHANGE OF IMAGE...

COSMETICS

...SHOW HIM THAT I'M STILL THE WANTON, EXCITING, LUSCIOUS WENCH HE MARRIED!—I SHALL EFFECT THE ULTIMATE TRANSFORMATION

BUT FIRST I MUST DO THE IMPOSSIBLE — GET A COUPLE OF HOURS TO MYSELF!

IT MUST BE MOTHER LOVE THAT MAKES THESE COOKIES TASTE SO GOOD....

I BEEN SAVING IT.

THAT'S IT!! NO MORE GUM!

BUT MA!

GOOD THING SHE DIDN'T FIND THE ONES ON THE DRESSER...

CAN I HAVE A COOKIE, MOM?
I GUESS SO...

CAN MY FRIENDS HAVE A COOKIE, MOM?
I GUESS SO...

HEY, GUYS! COOKIES!

IF YOU DON'T WANT PIGEONS... DON'T START FEEDING THEM.....

57

MICHAEL, IF YOU'RE RUDE TO ME ONCE MORE, YOU'LL GO TO YOUR ROOM FOR THE REST OF THE DAY— AND NO SUPPER!

BRRUPP!

THEY ALWAYS MAKE YOU CARRY OUT THE THREATS YOU WISH YOU HADN'T MADE.

MAYBE I COULD TAKE MICHAEL A LITTLE SUPPER....

HONEY, IF YOU SENT HIM TO BED WITHOUT SUPPER, YOU CAN'T GO BACK ON YOUR WORD.

BESIDES, HE'S A HEALTHY KID... HE SHOULD BE ABLE TO SURVIVE FOR ONE NIGHT.

YEAH... BUT I DON'T THINK I CAN.

I DON'T KNOW WHAT YOU'RE COMPLAINING ABOUT, CONNIE...

YOU'VE COMBINED PARENTHOOD WITH A CAREER, YOU MAKE THE DECISIONS, YOU GO OUT OR YOU DON'T GO OUT..

LET'S FACE IT. YOU'RE LIVING THE LIFE OF A TRULY LIBERATED WOMAN!

SOMETIMES LIBERATION STINKS.

CONNIE IS SO DEPRESSED. EVERY TIME I SEE HER I FEEL GUILTY. COMPARED TO HER... I HAVE EVERYTHING!

I HAVE A STABLE HOMELIFE, A FINE FAMILY, A RELIABLE, LOVING HUSBAND AND FATHER;... HOW COULD I EVER COMPLAIN?!

YEAH. TOO BAD THERE AREN'T MORE OF US TRULY GREAT GUYS TO GO AROUND....

GOOD GRIEF, WOULD YOU LOOK AT THE ADS IN THIS PAPER, ELLY!

IT'S ALL SWINGING COUPLES LOOKING FOR PARTNERS!

GOSH, I COULD NEVER IMAGINE DOING A THING LIKE THAT... COULD YOU, ANNE?

OF COURSE NOT!... I'D HAVE TO LOSE AT LEAST 20 POUNDS!

YOU WERE A DIFFERENT PERSON WHEN YOU WERE MARRIED, CONNIE...

YOU WERE A DEFEATIST... WHERE DID YOUR INFERIORITY COMPLEX GO?

HE LEFT ME WITH A HOUSE, A CAR, THE BILLS, TWO SIAMESE CATS AND A FIVE YEAR OLD KID.

JYNN

SLEEP TIGHT, BABY...

IT'S DONE... THE CLEANING, THE IRONING, THE WASH, THE BABY'S IN BED...

JYNN JOHNSTON

I'VE GOT SOME FREE TIME... AND I'D BETTER TAKE ADVANTAGE OF IT QUICKLY....

HI, MA! WHAT'S TO EAT?

...BECAUSE IT WON'T LAST LONG.

61

...BUT HOW LONG COULD I WEAR IT WITHOUT PASSING OUT..?

JUST LOOK AT THE BATHING SUITS THEY EXPECT US TO WEAR THIS YEAR!

EVEN IF I LOST 10 POUNDS I STILL COULDN'T LOOK LIKE THAT!

DON'T WORRY ABOUT IT, ELLY. THOSE BUSTY, WASP-WAISTED, THIN-LEGGED GIRLS ARE ALL DEFORMED.....

WE'RE NORMAL.

I'M TELLING YOU, ELLY - THESE JOGGING SUITS WILL HELP!

I'M NOT THE ATHLETIC TYPE, ANN... I FEEL SILLY.

ONCE WE GET ONTO THE STREET IN THESE-- WE'LL REALLY FEEL LIKE RUNNING

...'CAUSE IF YOU'RE WALKING, YOU LOOK LIKE AN IDIOT.

OF COURSE I'M GOING TO TRAIN LIZZIE, MOM — I JUST DON'T THINK SHE'S READY FOR IT YET!

YES, I DO HAVE A POTTIE... SHE JUST WON'T SIT ON IT. — SURE IT'S A REGULAR ONE. NO, IT'S NOT TOO BIG...

I'D SAY IT WAS A PERFECT FIT.

GARLLDDPP?

YAH!

KACHUNG!

WHAT DO YOU MEAN — IT'S ONLY DOLLY PARTON!!

I TOOK LAWRENCE IN TO SEE JOHN, TODAY. — BOY, ARE THE GIRLS IN HIS OFFICE GORGEOUS!

ISN'T IT HARD ON YOU KNOWING HE'S WORKING WITH THEM ALL DAY?

— I MEAN HOW CAN YOU COMPETE WITH ALL THAT ICING?

.. BY BEING THE CAKE.

LYNN JOHNSTON

66

NAAH, LIZZIE... I GOT A **COOKIE** AN' YOU CAN'T HAAAVE ONE...

YBWL AAAH! MAA-MA!

~YUMM~SMACK.. GOOOD CookIEEE

UH UH UH! **COOKIE!**

MA! I TAUGHT LIZZIE A NEW WORD !!

HELLO? ELLY! WHERE ARE YOU?... YOU RAN OUT OF GAS?

YOU IDIOT! HOW COULD YOU DO A DUMB THING LIKE THAT!

COME AND GET YOU?.. NO.. I CAN'T.... WELL... BECAUSE...

..BECAUSE I LOCKED MY KEYS IN THE OTHER CAR...

ALL I HAVE TO DO IS **LOOK** AT MY MOM AND SHE GETS MAD!

HONEST, MIKE? YOU WERE JUST LOOKIN' AT HER?

YEAH. SHE WAS IN THE BATH AT THE TIME.

I'M GLAD YOU'RE GETTING OUT ON YOUR OWN TONIGHT, ELLY.

YOU'VE GOT TO GET AWAY FROM THE HOUSE—BE FREE... TO BE YOUR-SELF. BESIDES, WE NEED SOME FUN!

IF I CAN BE OF ANY HELP... MY PERSONAL HOME PHONE NUMBER IS 246-0013.

SEE?...NOTHING DOES MORE FOR YOUR SELF CONFIDENCE THAN A LITTLE TEMPTATION.

THAT WAITER ACTUALLY MADE A PASS AT ME, CONNIE. I MUST HAVE BEEN ACTING SINGLE OR SOMETHING.

DON'T TELL ME YOU'RE FEELING GUILTY BECAUSE SOME MAN THOUGHT YOU WERE ATTRACTIVE TONIGHT!

I'LL BET JOHN HAS ALL KINDS OF OPPORTUNITIES AT THIS CONVENTION OF HIS...

—AND I SAID SOMETHING WRONG, DIDN'T I?

I WISH DADDY WOULD HURRY UP AN' COME HOME...

I MISS DADDY, TOO, MICHAEL. WE'RE JUST NOT A FAMILY WITHOUT HIM.

WE DON'T REALIZE HOW MUCH WE NEED OUR DADDY UNTIL HE'S NOT HERE.

IS THAT WHY HE GOES AWAY SOMETIMES?

BOY, THAT WAS SOME SHIN-DIG!.. I GOT BLASTED!.. I MEAN HAMMERED, POLLUTED AND SMASHED!! HIC!

YOU KNOW, EL... IT'SH A DARNED GOOD THING I'M NOT A MALE CHAUVINIST MACHO-TYPE...

WATCH YOUR STEP...

SOME GUYS INSISHT ON BEING THE PROTECTOR AND THE SHUPERIOR MEMBER OF THE DUET...

THANK GOD I'M NOT TOO (BURP) PROUD TO BE CHAUFFEURED BY MY WIFE.

JYNN JOHNSTON

I'M GLAD YOU HAD SUCH A GOOD TIME TONIGHT, JOHN... ...JOHN?..

I GOT STUCK BETWEEN HAZEL AND LORRAINE WHO DISCUSSED EVERYTHING FROM THEIR HOUSEKEEPER'S BREATH TO LEGWAXING.

I'M ABSOLUTELY EXHAUSTED. ..I MUST HAVE FEIGNED INTEREST FOR AT LEAST FOUR SOLID HOURS!

JYNN JOHNSTON

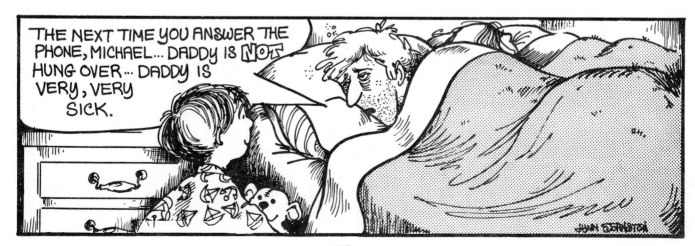

THE NEXT TIME YOU ANSWER THE PHONE, MICHAEL... DADDY IS **NOT** HUNG OVER... DADDY IS VERY, VERY SICK.

LYNN JOHNSTON

WHAT'S THE MATTER, JOHN... WHAT ARE ALL THESE PAPERS?

EVERY YEAR!—IT NEVER FAILS!—AS SOON AS YOU SEND OFF YOUR INCOME TAX FORMS...

—AS SOON AS IT'S TOO LATE...

YOU FIND ANOTHER DRAWER FULL OF DEDUCTIONS!!

—SO YOU WENT OUT AND JOINED A WEIGHT CONTROL CLINIC!

YEAH. I GO ONCE A WEEK AND I PAY $3.00 EACH TIME 'TILL I REACH MY GOAL.

I HOPE STEVE'S GIVING YOU SOME ENCOURAGEMENT, ANNE.

—HE FIGURES—AT $3.00 A WEEK, WITH MY WILL-POWER... I'M WORTH AT LEAST $45.00 A POUND.

WELL... HOW WAS YOUR COFFEEKLATCH WITH ANNE AND HER CRONIES?

WAIT A MINUTE—YOU THINK OUR COFFEE-KLATCHES ARE A WASTE OF TIME, DON'T YOU!

I DIDN'T EXACTLY MEAN IT LIKE THAT!... BUT WHAT ELSE WOULD YOU CALL IT!

HUMAN CONTACT.

For Better or For Worse
By Lynn Johnston

ARE WE NOT GOING TO SEE THAT LOVELY SMILE, MELISSA?

CERTAINLY... BY ALL MEANS LET ME KNOW IF YOU FEEL ANY PAIN!

THOSE SUPPLIES YOU NEEDED IMMEDIATELY HAVE BEEN BACK-ORDERED TILL NEXT MONTH, JOHN.

...AND LET'S JUST KEEP HIM HOME 'TILL HE'S OVER THIS BITING HABIT...

HONK HONK SCREECH TAXI! BLAAATTT HONK

MOM! MOM! DADDY'S HOME!

HI, DADDY...

GROWL

For Better or For Worse
By Lynn Johnston

FOR EASTER IS NOT A TIME FOR SADNESS, BUT A TIME FOR REJOICING. JUST AS SPRING AWAKENS SLEEPING FLOWERS AND ANIMALS AFTER A LONG, COLD WINTER, SO EASTER AWAKENS US TO THE WONDERS AND THE LOVE ALL AROUND....

IS CHURCH OPEN EVERY SUNDAY, MOM?

YES, MICHAEL.

THEN HOWCOME WE ONLY COME TWICE A YEAR?

...I WAS WONDERING IF YOU COULD TELL ME HOW MUCH I HAVE IN ACCOUNT NO. 01-632?

CHECKS WRITTEN?...OH, I'VE SPENT-SAY $280.00 GIVE OR TAKE $10.00 SINCE THE LAST STATEMENT.

YES-BUT I KEEP FOR-GETTING TO WRITE THEM DOWN. OH. YEAH, SURE, OK... THANKS. 'BYE.

DUMB BANKS.

WHAT IS IT, LIZZIE? SOMETHING HURTS? SORE TUMMY?

NO PINS, NO FEVER... IS IT TEETH, LIZZIE? ARE YOU HUNGRY?

WHAT'S THE MATTER, BABY, TELL ME!-TELL ME!

-WHY AREN'T THEY ALL BORN SPEAKING ENGLISH...

I HAD AN AWFUL NIGHT WITH THE KIDS, MOM. I WAS UP EVERY HALF HOUR!

-YEAH, FIRST ONE, THEN THE OTHER. YOU DON'T GET A CHANCE TO EVEN THINK ABOUT YOURSELF.

-I GUESS YOU WENT THROUGH ALL THIS WITH PHIL AND ME, DIDN'T YOU.

..ER..MOM.....DID WE EVER THANK YOU?

WE'RE LUCKY TO HAVE THE CHOICE OF HAVING OR NOT HAVING MORE KIDS, ELLY.

MY MOTHER REALLY HAD HER HANDS FULL—I WAS THE YOUNGEST OF 6 GIRLS!

YOUR MOM MUST HAVE **WANTED** A LARGE FAMILY, CONNIE.

—NOT EXACTLY, I WAS MY FATHER'S LAST TRY FOR A BOY.

IF WOMEN RESENT THEIR POSITION, THEY HAVE ONLY THEMSELVES TO BLAME.

IF MEN WERE ONLY TAUGHT AS BOYS TO DO THINGS FOR THEMSELVES—THIS PROBLEM WOULDN'T EXIST...

LYNN JOHNSTON

HEY, MOM.. COULD YOU GET ME A GLASS OF MILK?

SURE, MIKE... AS SOON AS I GET YOUR ROOM CLEANED UP.

I THINK I HAVE A CREDIT CARD...NO, WAIT, MAYBE I'VE GOT A CHECK...

—CAN I GET A DOLLAR AND 80¢ WORTH OF REGULAR, PLEASE?'

WHY DOES THIS THING ONLY RUN OUT OF GAS WHEN I'VE GOT IT!

LYNN

THE FUEL COMPANY DIDN'T OVER CHARGE US, ELLY - YOU PAID THEIR BILL TWICE! - THIS IS A CREDIT BALANCE.

NO WONDER THEY DIDN'T UNDER-STAND YOUR COMPLAINT. - IT SAYS RIGHT HERE "DO NOT PAY".

- I JUST PAY THE BILLS ... I'M NOT EXPECTED TO READ THEM!

LYNN JOHNSTON

PETE'S BEEN GONE A YEAR NOW, CONNIE - YOU'VE GOT TO ACCEPT THAT.

I KNOW. STILL- WHEN IT'S THE ONLY RELATION-SHIP I'VE HAD, IT'S HARD TO FORGET.

- OUR MARRIAGE WAS LIKE THE AGONY AND THE ECSTASY...

- I JUST WISH I COULD FORGET THE ECSTASY.

LYNN

DO YOU KNOW THAT CONNIE STILL COLORS HER HAIR BECAUSE OF PETER?

THAT RAT WOULDN'T HAVE STAYED IF SHE'D HAD PLASTIC SURGERY!

FOR HIM, SHE BECAME AN ARTSY, ATHLETIC RED-HEAD, A KITCHEN GENIUS AND A MODEL WIFE!

I ALWAYS WONDERED WHAT HE HAD THAT I DIDN'T HAVE.

LYNN

MOM! DAD!

NOW, MICHAEL, YOU TAKE THIS BAG, I'LL TAKE YOUR SUITCASE....

YOU TAKE ELLY'S LUGGAGE, DEAR—AND WE'LL LEAVE HER TO PICK UP THE BABY'S THINGS.

DO I REALLY GET TO SLEEP IN THE SAME BED MOM SLEPT IN WHEN SHE WAS LITTLE, GRAMPA?

YEP!—YOUR MOM SLEPT HERE, DREAMED HERE, DID HER THINKING HERE...

-SIGH-

...FOR AN OLDEN DAYS BED, IT FEELS PRETTY GOOD!

MOM, WHEN I WAS HERE BEFORE CHRISTMAS, YOU SPENT A WEEK LECTURING ME...

THIS TIME, WITH THE KIDS ... OUR RELATIONSHIP IS SO DIFFERENT!

MAYBE THAT'S BECAUSE ALONE—YOU'RE MY DAUGHTER...

-BUT WITH THE KIDS— WE'RE BOTH MOMS.

I MUST SAY — I DO ENJOY BEING A GRANDMA, ELLY!

I'M FREE TO LOVE AND SPOIL THESE TWO — THEN GIVE THEM BACK WHEN THEY'RE TIRED!

NO SLEEPLESS NIGHTS, NO DIAPERS, NO MESS, NO BABYSITTERS, NO TEARS...

OH, WHY DID THOSE WONDERFUL YEARS GO BY SO FAST?

AW, COME ON, MIKE — YOU'RE TOO OLD TO WANT A TEDDY BEAR ANY-WAYS!

BUT, GRAMPA, I NEED SUPERTEDDY! — I TALK TO HIM EVERY NIGHT!

MICHAEL! BIG BOYS KNOW THAT TEDDYS DON'T TALK!

··I KNOW. BUT HE LISTENS.

YOU KNOW, MOM, I THOUGHT GETTING MARRIED WOULD MAKE ME GROW UP.

BUT NOW I'M A MOTHER AND I STILL FEEL AND ACT LIKE A CHILD!

WHEN DOES THE DAY COME THAT YOU ACTUALLY BECOME A MATURE ADULT?

I DON'T KNOW. I'M OVER 60, AND I'M STILL WAITING!

HI THERE, MIKE—WHAT DO YOU SAY WE READ A BOOK?

YOU CAN WATCH THAT ANY DAY!—HOW OFTEN DO YOU AND I READ A STORY?

WELL, I SEE GRAMPA HASN'T LOST HIS TOUCH!

—BECAUSE GRAMPA JUST THREATENED TO BLOW UP THE T.V.

YOU REALLY SHOULD STOP SMOKING, DAD—IT WOULD BE BETTER FOR YOUR HEALTH!

DO YOU HAVE TO WEAR BLUE ALL THE TIME, MOM?—AND WHY DON'T YOU CHANGE YOUR HAIR?

WE'VE ALWAYS BEEN SORRY YOU DIDN'T FINISH UNIVERSITY BEFORE GETTING MARRIED, ELLY...

I WONDERED HOW LONG IT WOULD TAKE BEFORE WE RESUMED OUR OLD PARENT-DAUGHTER ROLES...

SIGH...YOU'LL BE BACK IN TORONTO SOON.—THESE VISITS ARE JUST TOO SHORT.

SEEMS LIKE YESTERDAY YOU WERE AS SMALL AS ELIZABETH.

YOU STILL THINK OF ME AS YOUR LITTLE GIRL, DON'T YOU, DAD?

NO—BUT IF YOU'RE ALLOWED TO GROW UP, I'M ALLOWED TO GET MUSHY ABOUT IT.

"WHEW~ WHAT A TRIP! -IT'S SURE GOOD TO BE HOME!"

JOHN... YOU CLEANED UP THE ENTIRE HOUSE!

SOME THINGS ONE DOES AS A MEANS TO SURVIVAL...

SO, HOW DID YOU LIKE BEING A BACHELOR FOR TWO WEEKS?

OH ...IT WAS O.K. FOR A WHILE...

WHAT DID YOU MISS THE MOST?

THE CHAOS.

CONNIE CAME BY LAST WEEK. -SHE WAS ALL LONELY AND DEPRESSED.

I WISH I COULD HAVE SAID SOMETHING TO CHEER HER UP...

-HECK,-I DON'T KNOW ANYTHING ABOUT CRAZY, EMOTIONAL NUT-CASES!

-SO I TOLD HER TO WAIT TILL YOU CAME HOME.

YOUR LITTLE CHRISTOPHER IS GROWING LIKE A WEED, ANNE!

IT'S BECAUSE I DON'T GIVE HIM COMMERCIAL FOODS! —I MAKE EVERYTHING MYSELF!

—AND I THINK MOTHERS WHO BUY PROCESSED FOODS ARE IGNORING THE...

—IT'S FROM A REPUTABLE BAKERY...

SOMETIMES I FEEL SO BORED WITH MY LIFE, ANNE...

I CAN'T SEE GETTING A JOB—BUT I'VE GOT TO DO SOMETHING!

WELL, THERE'S ALWAYS ONE THING YOU CAN DO IF YOUR LIFE SEEMS DULL...

—HAVE ANOTHER KID.

ANOTHER KID!?—WE'RE NOT HAVING ANOTHER BABY, ELLY!

ARE YOU POSITIVE? ABSOLUTELY POSITIVE!

THEN I GUESS IT'S TIME YOU TOOK SOME PERMANENT PRECAUTIONS...

I'M NOT THAT POSITIVE!!!

HOUSING COSTS AND SOARING FUEL PRICES ARE CRUSHING THE HOPES OF MANY YOUNG COUPLES WHO- CLICK!

"A GROUP OF STUDENTS ARE PICKETING THE UNIVERSITY TO PROTEST THE LACK OF OPPORTUNITY IN THE THEY CLAIM THEY ARE OVERQUAL FOR JOBS AVA

SCIENTISTS WARN THAT IRREPARABLE DAMAGE HAS ALREADY BEEN DONE TO THE ATMOSPHERE THROUGH THE INDISCRIMINANT USE OF POLLU

MOM?.... WILL THERE BE ANYTHING LEFT FOR ME?

FLOWERS!-THANK YOU, MICHAEL!-WHERE DID YOU FIND THEM?

WELL, I SORT OF...ER...GOT THEM FROM MISS BAIRD'S PLACE.

YOU CAN'T GO TAKING FLOWERS FROM PEOPLE'S GARDENS, HONEY-IT'S VERY WRONG.-YOU MUST NEVER DO IT AGAIN!

...BUT IF YOU DO-TRY AND LEAVE ON THE STEM.

CAN I PLAY IN THE SPRINKLER, MOM? NO!

BUT IT'S HOT OUT AND I'M NOT SICK OR ANYTHING! I SAID NO!

THAT'S NOT FAIR! THERE'S NO REASON WHY I CAN'T PLAY IN THE SPRINKLER!

I KNOW...BUT ONCE YOU'VE SAID NO...YOU'VE GOT TO SAVE FACE.

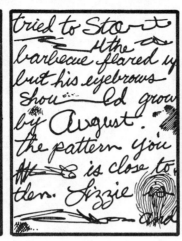

SHRIEK! PUT DOWN THAT BRUSH!!

WITH A CLOSET FULL OF PAINT-COVERED CLOTHES, HE WEARS A NEW SHIRT!

YOU GO AND CHANGE... -RIGHT NOW!

GEE!-IF I DO IT FAST CAN I HAVE A COOKIE, MOM?

I THINK I DESERVE BETTER THAN THAT!

DON'T YOU WORRY ABOUT BEING OVER 30, ANNE?-I CAN'T HELP THINKING HOW OLD I LOOK.

AT ONE TIME, I'D WALK DOWN THE STREET, CONSTRUCTION WORKERS WOULD WHISTLE AT ME.-I WISH THEY WOULD NOW!

-OF COURSE I WOULD STILL EYE THEM WITH CONTEMPT....

CONSIDERING I'M OVER 30, JOHN, I'VE DECIDED TO BE VERY OBJECTIVE ABOUT MY LOOKS.

SO... ON A SCALE OF 1 TO 10, I'D SAY I'M 7... WHAT DO YOU THINK? - OR AM I 6?... (THERE ARE ODD DAYS I'M 8....)

WELL?

IF YOU THINK I'M FALLING INTO THAT TRAP, YOU'RE CRAZY!

IF THERE WAS A BOMB DROPPED ON US, DADDY... WOULD WE GO TO HEAVEN?

WOULD HEAVEN GET FILLED UP? - WOULD EVERYONE TURN INTO ANGELS?

- AND WHAT ABOUT THE PEOPLE WHO DROPPED THE BOMB? - WOULD THEY BE ALONE IN THE WHOLE EARTH?

MIKE... CAN WE GO BACK TO "WHY IS THE SKY BLUE?"

THERE'S GOTTA BE A REASON WHY BOYS ARE DIFFERENT FROM GIRLS!

I ASKED MY MOM ONCE... BUT SHE WOULDN'T TELL ME.

... I GUESS WE JUST GOT DIFFERENT DECORATIONS.

YOUR LITTLE WIFEY JUST GOT INTO A SIZE 10— SO THERE!

THAT'S GREAT, ELLY— LET'S SEE...

HEY- THIS SAYS SIZE 12!

I JUST SAID I GOT INTO A SIZE 10-I DIDN'T SAY I COULD WEAR IT!

WHY IS IT THAT WE ARE EXPECTED TO RETAIN OUR FIGURES WHILE OUR MEN CAN GO TO POT?

WE SPEND YEARS IN THE KITCHEN, WE GET PREGNANT, AND YET WE'RE STILL SUPPOSED TO LOOK LIKE SYLPHS!

WHY IS IT THAT A PAUNCH IS FINE ON A MAN, BUT IS UGLY ON A GIRL WHO'S HAD TWO! KIDS!

RIGHT.- IF ANYONE DESERVES TO BE FAT,— WE DO.

I'M SORRY YOU'RE NOT FEELING WELL, HONEY.

I TOOK LIZZIE TO THE SITTER, AND MIKE IS IN CRAFT CLASS.

I CAN PICK UP LIZZIE... BUT THERE'S NO WAY I CAN GET DOWN TO COLLECT MICHAEL.

...SO, THAT MEANS I CAN BE SICK UNTIL 11:45.

BRAWLING O'BRIAN IS HERE WITH AN EMERGENCY TOOTH ACHE, JOHN.

—WELL, COME RIGHT IN MR. ER— O'BRIAN.

—NOT SO FAST, DOC.—

—I'M SCARED!!

WHY DOES EVERYONE HATE DENTISTS, JEAN? THEY SEE MY OFFICE AS AN EXPENSIVE TORTURE CHAMBER

WE'RE JUST PEOPLE AND WE'RE UNFAIRLY STEREOTYPED!—I'M A NICE GUY—BUT I'M STUCK WITH THIS BAD IMAGE!

—YOU COULD HAVE STUDIED SOMETHING ELSE.—LAW FOR EXAMPLE.

NAH!—LAWYERS ARE ALL CROOKS.

CHEW GULP! GOBBLE CHOMP GULP!

WHERE ARE YOUR MANNERS, MICHAEL!

YOU'RE EATING LIKE A PIG!! NOW SLOW DOWN!

BUT IT'S LIVER & SPINACH MA!..IF I SLOW DOWN I'LL TASTE IT!!

THERE'S ONE DONUT IN THE FRIDGE.... I CAN'T STOP THINKING ABOUT IT.

I'VE GOT TO KEEP AWAY FROM IT. I DON'T NEED IT. I MUST HAVE **WILL POWER!**

I CAN'T TAKE IT ANY MORE. **I GIVE UP!!**

¡GASP¡.. ONE LAST DESPERATE BURST OF RESISTANCE.

Lynn

I'M BREAKING DOWN. AGAIN. I'M GOING TO OPEN THE FRIDGE DOOR.

THIS IS IT. I'M TOO WEAK TO RESIST TEMPTATION!

I'VE THROWN OUT MY DIGNITY AND MY SELF-RESPECT FOR A LOUSY DONUT...

AND IT'S **GONE!**

Lynn

HAPPY BIRTHDAY, MOM! — I WRAPPED THIS ALL BY MYSELF!

I CHOSE IT ALL BY MYSELF AN' I MADE THE CARD ALL BY MYSELF!

IT'S LOVELY, MICHAEL!

THANK YOU.

LYNN

I HEAR YOU GAVE ELLY A MICRO-WAVE OVEN!

POKE PROD

YEP! — THE KIND THAT DOES EVERYTHING BUT SAY GRACE.

SHE'S GOING TO LOVE COOKING WITH THAT!

YEAH. NOW SHE CAN BURN DINNER IN ONE TENTH THE TIME!

LYNN

JOHN!—YOU'RE NOT GOING OUTSIDE LIKE THAT!

ORANGE AND BLUE PLAID WITH GREEN HOUNDS-TOOTH CHECK— AAACK!!

HONESTLY! WHAT WILL PEOPLE THINK?

WITH LUCK, THEY'LL THINK I'M A MAN FIXING A FENCE.

YOU'RE HENPECKED! IF YOUR WIFE BUGS YOU ABOUT YOUR CLOTHES—

—TELL HER OFF! TELL HER YOU'LL WEAR WHAT YOU LIKE!

TELL HER IF SHE'S NOT HAPPY, TO GO TAKE A FLYING LEAP!

THEN AGAIN... I COULD CHANGE.

TED SAYS I'M BEING HENPECKED. HE SAYS I SHOULD WEAR WHAT I LIKE!

YOU CAN'T TAKE ADVICE FROM TED. HE'S A BACHELOR AND AN IDIOT!

THAT MAY BE—BUT THE MAN STILL KNOWS A HENPECK WHEN HE SEES ONE!!

HE LIVES WITH HIS MOTHER.

I NEVER COMPLAINED ABOUT PETE'S CLOTHES...

HE WAS A PERFECT DRESSER.—ALWAYS IN THE LATEST STYLE.

HIS CLOTHES WERE PERFECT, HIS HAIR WAS PERFECT—HE LOOKED FANTASTIC!

— LIKE THAT THIN PLYWOOD WITH THE WALNUT VENEER.

YACK YACK YACK YACK YACK YA...

SLAM!

...ACK YACK YACK YACK YACK YACK...

SO I TOOK A BITE OUT OF THE DUMB CREAM CHEESE. SO WHAT!

—I GUESS I SHOULDA TOLD HER THE TRUTH.

HOW DID I KNOW SHE'D RECOGNIZE MY TEETH PRINTS!

WHAT'S THE TROUBLE, LIZZIE?

YOUR BUNNY? WHAT'S THE MATTER WITH YOUR BUNNY?

ELLY?—WHAT'S WRONG WITH LIZZIE'S BUNNY?

I WASHED IT.

I SHOULD LET THIS PLACE GO TO POT... THAT'D SHOW THEM!

—LET THE LAUNDRY PILE UP, LET THE SINKS GROW FUNGUS, LET THE DISHES LIE!

—THE ONLY TIME THEY NOTICE THAT I DO SOMETHING AROUND HERE...

—IS WHEN THEY FIND SOMETHING I *HAVEN'T* DONE!

FRYPAN Magic

WHEW! TALK ABOUT LONG DAYS! — AM I GLAD THIS ONE'S OVER!

ALL YOUR DISILLUSIONS ABOUT HOME & PARENTING DON'T EVEN COMPARE TO THE WAY I FEEL ABOUT DENTISTRY, SOMETIMES, ELLY...

I HAD A KID IN TODAY WHO NOT ONLY BIT MY ASSISTANT— BUT SPENT THE ENTIRE APPOINTMENT COUNTING MY NOSE HAIRS.

MAMA! DID YOU SEW UP TEDDY'S NOSE?

YOU SHOULDN'T HAVE! NOW TEDDY HATH TO DALK LIKE NITH!

ELLY DOESN'T THINK I UNDERSTAND HER (GAUZE, PLEASE...) BUT I DO!

SHE THINKS THAT I DON'T THINK ABOUT WHAT SHE'S THINKING ABOUT... BUT I DO!

(FORCEPS)... I JUST DON'T HAVE AS MUCH TIME AS SHE DOES TO THINK ABOUT WHAT SHE'S THINKING ABOUT.

OH, MICHAEL! I STILL CAN'T BELIEVE YOU'RE IN GRADE ONE!

THE NEXT TWELVE WILL BE THE BEST YEARS OF YOUR LIFE, HONEY.

I DON'T THINK SCHOOL IS GOING TO BE AS GREAT AS YOU SAY, MOM.

...THEY'RE MAKING US **WORK!**

NO, MICHAEL, WE ARE NOT GOING TO BUY A DOG -AND THAT'S THAT!

BUT, WHY, MOM! WHY CAN'T WE GET A DOG? **WHY?**

FOR ONE THING.... I CAN'T EVEN RAISE A PLANT.

THE HOUSE IS SURE QUIET WITHOUT MICHAEL. THE WHOLE PLACE SEEMS STRANGE!

WITH HIM IN SCHOOL ALL DAY, LIFE IS DIFFERENT... EASIER .... PEACEFUL...

HOW LONG AM I GOING TO FEEL GUILTY FOR ENJOYING IT?

JUST A COUPLE OF DAYS BEFORE OUR CAMPING TRIP, ANNE!

OUTSIDE IN A TENT, WITH A CAMP STOVE, AN OUTHOUSE, NO RUNNING WATER, NO T.V.— THE KIDS WILL LOVE IT!

... AT LEAST THAT'S WHAT WE KEEP TELLING OURSELVES.

Lynn

A WEEKEND CAMPING— JUST THINK ABOUT IT!

RUSHING RIVERS, FRESH AIR, THE AUTUMN LEAVES...

IT'S THE SORT OF THING THAT MAKES TWO PEOPLE FALL IN LOVE AGAIN!

CAN I WATCH?

Lynn

NO, I'M FINE, HONEY, I'M FINE!....REALLY, I'M NOT TIRED.

NO, NO...YOU DON'T HAVE TO DRIVE!

JUST RELAX AND AMUSE THE KIDS!

119

I'M TAKIN' LIZZIE ACROSS THE STREET, MA!

OK, WATCH FOR CARS! - LOOK BOTH WAYS! - QUICKLY, NOW...

I CAN SEE THE EMPTY NEST ALREADY.

YOU PLAY GENTLY WITH BABY, MICHAEL. - CATCH, LIZZIE!

GOOD GIRL! - NOW TOSS IT TO DADDY...

TOSS TO DADDY, BABY...THROW THE BALL TO...

WHAP

- WITH MICHAEL IN SCHOOL, I GUESS ELLY WILL BE GETTING A JOB!

WELL, I HOPE THE SUBJECT DOESN'T COME UP.

I'M NOT HOLDING HER BACK, MIND YOU - SHE CAN BE AS LIB- -ERATED AS THE REST OF THEM!

...AS LONG AS SHE DOES IT AT HOME.

EITHER I HAVE TOO MUCH EDUCATION FOR MOST OF THESE JOBS OR I DON'T HAVE ENOUGH!

IF I DID DECIDE TO WORK I COULD ALWAYS BE A CLERK OR A WAITRESS.

BUT I REALLY WANT A CHALLENGING CAREER IN MY FIELD OF INTEREST!

- IF I CAN REMEMBER WHAT IT IS....

I KNOW IT'S SELFISH, BUT I LIKE MY WIFE TO BE WHERE SHE IS.

I DON'T LIKE THE IDEA OF WORKING MOTHERS. A HOUSE SHOULD BE A HOME.

CALL ME NARROW MINDED... CALL ME OLD FASHIONED...

BUT OINK AT ME ONCE MORE AND YOU'RE FIRED!

JOHN, I'VE BEEN THINKING...

NOW THAT I HAVE MORE TIME, WHAT WOULD YOU SAY TO MY GETTING A PART-TIME JOB?

COME ON! - I CAN'T SPEND MY LIFE BAKING COOKIES AND PICKING UP SOCKS!

MY MOTHER DID!

SINCE YOU WANT TO WORK, HONEY...I HAVE A SUGGESTION.

JEAN IS TAKING A WEEK OFF-SO I'LL NEED AN ASSISTANT.

IT'S NOT EXCITING, BUT IT WOULD BE A CHANGE.

WHAT HAVE I DONE?

TEACHER DRAWS A WHOLE LOT BETTER THAN YOU, MOM.

YEAH... AN' SHE PRINTS BETTER THAN YOU TOO!

HOWCOME YOU CAN'T READ AS WELL AS TEACHER?

..I'VE BEEN DEMOTED.

UH! COOKIE! NUM-NUM! COOKIE GOOD. NIZZIE EAT COOKIE!

SHE'S GROWING UP, ELLY... SHE'S WALKING AND TALKING AND TURNING INTO A REAL LITTLE GIRL.

LET'S HOPE I'VE GOT A FEW YEARS BEFORE SHE FINDS ANOTHER BOYFRIEND!

LOOK, ANNE, I BOUGHT THIS TO WEAR IN THE CLINIC.

WHAT DO YOU THINK?

I WON'T HAVE TO WEAR THE STUFF I WEAR AROUND THE HOUSE FOR A WHOLE WEEK!

..IN OTHER WORDS, YOU'VE EXCHANGED ONE UNIFORM FOR ANOTHER!

CHRISTOPHER WILL LOVE HAVING ELIZABETH HERE, ELLY!

MIKE WILL COME OVER AFTER SCHOOL, AND WE'LL BE A BIG FAMILY!

THEY'LL BE IN GOOD HANDS, SO RELAX. A CHANGE OF SCENE WILL DO YOU GOOD.

SHE THINKS I'M IRRESPONSIBLE.

ELLY, DENTISTRY IS AN EXACTING BUSINESS. — I GET VERY TENSE.

SO I GOT IMPATIENT. MAYBE I BARKED AT YOU A FEW TIMES...

SO WHAT IF I SAID YOU WERE A KLUTZ AND A DUMMY!

DO YOU HAVE TO TAKE IT PERSONALLY?

LYNN

OOPS! — I'D BETTER CLEAN THAT PLASTER OFF THE FLOOR OR JOHN WILL THROW A FIT!

YOUR HUSBAND IS FANATIC ABOUT KEEPING THIS PLACE CLEAN AND TIDY. — HE GOES NUTS IF WE LEAVE A MESS ANYWHERE!

ELLY, THIS IS NO TIME TO DISCUSS WHERE I THREW MY SOCKS THIS MORNING!

LYNN

BOY, WHAT A DAY! I'M GLAD THE WEEK'S OVER.

YEAH! I'M ABSOLUTELY EXHAUSTED!

WORKING FULL TIME REALLY TAKES IT OUT OF YOU. IT'S SO GOOD TO BE HOME.

WELL... WHAT'S FOR SUPPER?

LYNN

126